ARE THE HORIZONTAL
LINES PARALLEL,
OR DO THEY SLOPE?

FIND OUT ON PAGE 78

NATIONAL
GEOGRAPHIC
KiDS

FEATURING
CHALLENGES FROM THE
NATIONAL GEOGRAPHIC
CHANNEL HIT
BRAIN GAMES

BRAIN GAMES

THE MIND-BLOWING SCIENCE OF YOUR AMAZING BRAIN

JENNIFER SWANSON
FOREWORD BY HANK GREEN

CONTENTS

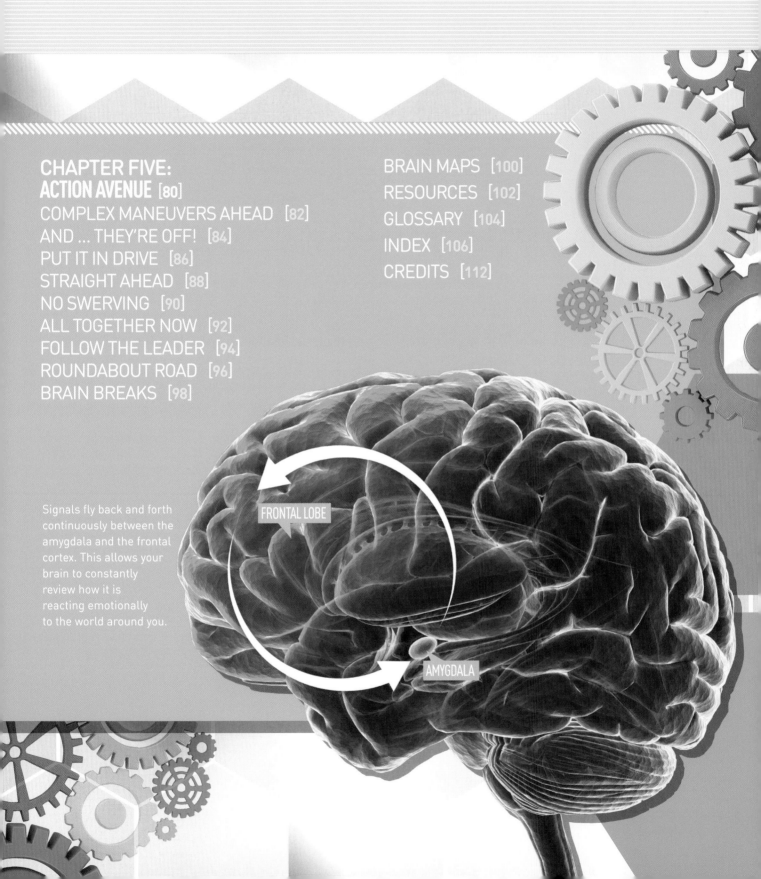

Signals fly back and forth continuously between the amygdala and the frontal cortex. This allows your brain to constantly review how it is reacting emotionally to the world around you.

FRONTAL LOBE

AMYGDALA

FOREWORD

YOUR BRAIN PROBABLY WEIGHS ABOUT THREE POUNDS. I DON'T KNOW ABOUT YOU, BUT I CAN EAT MORE THAN THREE POUNDS OF PIZZA IN A SINGLE SITTING.

It just isn't a very big thing. For every pound of brain, the average adult person has more than 50 pounds of other stuff ... bones and organs and skin and toenails. We're mostly not brain, but at the same time we're actually all brain. There's the stuff we're made of, our bodies, and then there's who we are. That stuff, what you like, what you know, the things that have happened to you— that's all brain.

How? Well, it's complicated.

In fact, some scientists have said that your brain is the most complicated object in the known universe, outside of other human brains, of course. What a marvelous thing to have discovered. That all this time, just sitting between your ears, there's a lump of fat and nervous tissue that somehow stores all of your memories and your skills and your wishes and your wants and your fears and your favorite stuff. And, of all the things we have discovered and studied in our quest to understand the universe, it is the most complex thing there is.

If you take a step back and think about it, your average trip to the grocery store is just a bunch of these three-pound lumps wandering around the aisles looking for stuff to feed themselves.

And brains have to continually seek out food because a brain is a hungry beast. While the brain is less than 2 percent of the average person's body weight, 20 percent of our calories are burned by the brain. Thinking takes a lot of energy!

And since we evolved in a world of far more limited resources than we have now, we aren't designed to just waste energy willy-nilly. No, if brains need a ton of extra food for their upkeep, it's because they're using that energy to do important things. Things like finding food, forming friendships, solving problems, and maybe, most important, sharing information between individuals (which, by the way, is what I'm doing right now).

With your brain burning through lunch faster than any other part of our body, you ought to be using that power to its full potential. And I can think of no better use than to apply the brain to the study of the brain. Aside from just being fascinating, it will help us cure diseases, prolong our lives, and maybe even expand what the human species is capable of.

Of course, the really weird thing about all this is that the brain is doing the learning, and it's the brain you're learning about. Using your brain to study your brain? Now that's a challenge.

HANK GREEN
HOST, *SciSHOW*
& *CRASHCOURSE*

INTRODUCTION:
MEET YOUR BRAIN

Your brain is the most powerful and complex supercomputer ever built. It's the one thing that makes you YOU! Your brain is mission control for the rest of your body. It sits in the driver's seat and steers you through life. You can't do anything without your brain. It's your boss. It runs the show and gives commands to your body for everything you do—even when you're asleep. Not bad for something about the size of a softball that looks like a wrinkled sponge.

So, fire up your neurons and hang on to your hippocampus. It's time to try some brain games on a rockin' ride through your cerebral superhighway.

Your brain is broken up into three main parts: the cerebrum, the cerebellum, and the brain stem. The biggest part of your brain is the cerebrum (suh-REE-brum), which takes up about 85 percent of your head. It's your brain's control system. Split in half, with two lobes on each side, it handles pretty much everything you do, along with the cerebellum (sair-uh-bell-um) and the brain stem. Thinking, feeling, sensing, making memories, and feeling emotions all happen here.

Put your hand on the back of your head, just below the bony part of your skull. Feel that? That's your cerebellum. It's responsible for all your body movement. The cerebellum controls balance and coordination. It's the reason why you can stand on one foot and not fall over.

The third part of the brain is the brain stem. It connects the brain to the spinal column and controls all those tasks you don't even think about—like breathing, heart rate, blood pressure, and digestion. You know, the stuff that keeps you alive.

Your brain is smarter and more complex than any supercomputer. It runs on less energy and never shuts down. Unlike most computers, though, your brain can learn. It is an efficient thinking machine. But how much do we really know about our complex cranium command system? Let's put your brain to the test to find out.

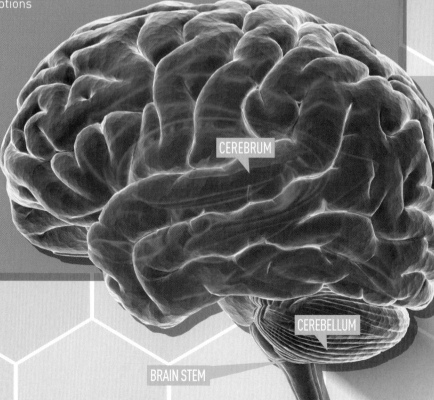

CEREBRUM

CEREBELLUM

BRAIN STEM

THE ENERGY USED BY THE BRAIN EVERY DAY IS ENOUGH TO LIGHT A 10-WATT BULB.

NEURO NOTES

Your cerebrum is divided into four lobes. Each has its own job:

FRONTAL LOBE handles judgment, insight, the ability to speak, personality, emotions, and some forms of memory.

OCCIPITAL LOBE manages sight.

PARIETAL LOBE controls sensory processing/touch, voluntary movement, and spatial awareness.

TEMPORAL LOBE handles hearing, speech comprehension, smell, taste, and memory.

INTRODUCTION:
HOW TO USE THIS BOOK

CHALLENGE

Solve this cube in less than 20 moves. Can you do it? Probably not. It's hard to do. Solving this complicated puzzle requires your brain to do several things at once.

PUT YOUR BRAIN TO THE TEST. READ THE **CHALLENGE** AND GIVE IT A TRY.

WHAT EXACTLY IS HAPPENING?

The Rubik's Cube requires your brain to use spatial reasoning. Spatial reasoning can also be called visual thinking. Your brain sees an image, such as each colored square, and then thinks about where that square needs to go to solve the puzzle. Some of that thinking takes place in the very back of your head. The occipital lobe, smallest of the four lobes of your cerebrum, is home to sight perception. It is where you process things that you see. You also recognize color here. But more happens than just seeing the cube. Spatial reasoning includes the ability to analyze things and solve complex problems, like this puzzle.

Your eyes see the colors on the square. The image is transmitted to the occipital lobe. Your brain uses its knowledge of movement to reason, or predict, how moving a square will affect the overall cube. As your fingers manipulate the cube, your brain evaluates each movement. It decides how to move next. If you give it enough time, you will solve the puzzle. Or not. It just depends on how much time you have.

THEN READ ABOUT **WHAT'S HAPPENING** IN YOUR BRAIN!

A+

CAN THE RUBIK'S CUBE IMPROVE OUR LIVES?

Two computer scientists at Northeastern University in Massachusetts, U.S.A., think so. As they see it, the Rubik's Cube is the ultimate puzzle. It has more than 43 quintillion answers. That's 43 followed by 18 zeros. In fact, one computer was tasked with trying them all. It took more than one year to do it. The question is: Why is this important?

Solving the Rubik's Cube was not earth-shattering in and of itself. It's how the computer did it. The scientists believe that the computer must break down each solution into subproblems. If those same thought processes were applied to bigger problems, like how to route planes safely or how to speed up phone calls and Internet connections, the effects on everyday human life would be pretty spectacular.

WANT TO KNOW MORE?
CHECK OUT THE **SIDEBARS.**

CHAPTER ONE

CRUISING ALONG THE
CEREBRAL SUPERHIGHWAY

When it comes to your brain, it's the thought that counts.
Ready to learn how your brain turns your senses
into thoughts? →

START YOUR ENGINES

Get ready, get set, and put your brain to work!

CHALLENGE

Jump up and down. Grab one foot and hold it in the air. Now spin around.

Were you able to follow all of those commands? Probably. The question is how you were able to do that. Your brain told you what to do.

WHAT EXACTLY IS HAPPENING?

Those were pretty complex instructions. Your brain had to read the words, process them into actions, and send a message to each muscle telling it what to do. It had to control your arms, legs, hands, and feet—all while keeping you upright and in balance. Whew! That's a lot of steps. If you were to program a robot to do all of those things, it would probably take a few days or even months to wire it together so that all the parts would work at the same time. Then you would have to write out all of those instructions for the robot. Your brain did it all in a few seconds. How is that possible?

Your brain has its very own communication system. It's called your neural network. The neural network is made up of more than 86 billion nerve cells, called neurons. Neurons stretch across your brain and form pathways. Microscopic bits of information zip along these pathways as fast as the fastest cars—that's 260 miles an hour (418 km/h)! Neurons are the worker bees of the brain. They transmit information via electrical impulse to muscles, glands, or even other neurons.

So when you read all of those instructions, your brain created a thought. A thought is an electrical signal that travels along a neuron cell pathway from one end to the other. Thoughts begin in the frontal lobe, the source of your intelligence. The frontal lobe's job is to plan and organize your thoughts. Neurons connect the frontal lobe via the cerebral superhighway to the part of the brain where input from your senses is processed, like the parietal lobe for the sense of touch. By combining the information from these lobes, the brain creates thoughts that tell you what to think and how to react to the world around us.

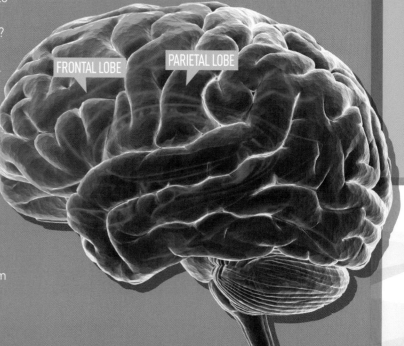

FRONTAL LOBE

PARIETAL LOBE

NEURO NOTES

Neurons are long cells that have three parts: **DENDRITES,** a **CELL BODY,** and an **AXON.** The dendrites are the collection center. Dendrites gather information and send it to the cell body. The cell body receives the information and then shoots it to the axon. The axon sends the message to another neuron and so on, until the information reaches the part of the brain where it is acted upon.

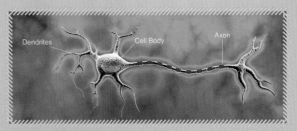

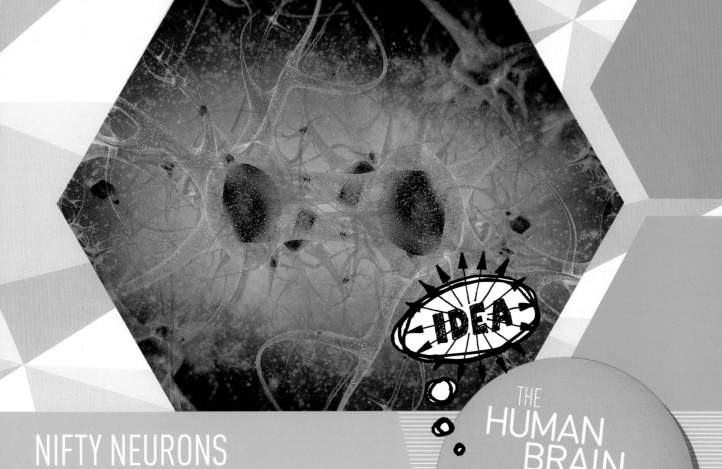

NIFTY NEURONS

Neurons are defined by the type of job they do:

SENSORY NEURONS take information from your senses and send it to the brain.

MOTOR NEURONS send information from the brain or spinal column to muscles and other organs.

INTERNEURONS act as the connection between the sensory and motor neurons.

Pretty nifty, right?

IDEA

THE **HUMAN BRAIN,** ON AVERAGE, PROCESSES **TENS OF THOUSANDS** OF THOUGHTS A DAY.

MIND MATTERS

WHAT A NERVE

MOTOR NEURONS ARE THE LONGEST CELLS IN THE BODY. Their cell bodies are located in the lower back. But their axons can stretch all the way from the base of the spine to your big toe. Motor neurons can reach about four feet (1.2 m) in length. That's just a little bit longer than a baseball bat.

SHORTCUTS AHEAD

Your brain is constantly bombarded with input. Information needs to be received and processed within seconds. So your brain takes shortcuts.

CHALLENGE

WHAT DO YOU SEE?

Two blue triangles and three dark circles, right? Wrong.

Neither the triangles nor the circles are really there.

To make sense of the picture, your brain told you they were present. But they really aren't. This is called an optical illusion.

[MIND MATTERS]

RIGHT VS. LEFT

THE RIGHT SIDE OF YOUR BRAIN IS YOUR CREATIVE SIDE. It helps you to be good at art and music. The left side of your brain is analytical. It helps you do things like problem solving, math, and writing.

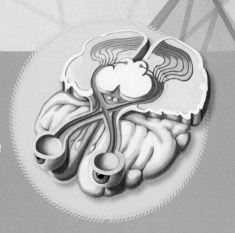

Your retina, a layer of tissue at the back of the eye, sees an image and translates it into an electrical impulse. The impulse travels along the optic nerve to your visual cortex. The visual cortex then identifies the image. Voilà! You see the image.

Did you know? What your right eye sees is processed in the left side of your visual cortex—and vice versa.

WHAT EXACTLY IS HAPPENING?

An optical illusion is a picture that uses color, light, or patterns to trick the brain into seeing something that isn't there.

Optical illusions show us that even though the brain has been fooled, it's working the way it's supposed to. Learning how the brain reacts to an optical illusion is a great way to get an inside look at how your brain works.

Your brain is constantly processing new input. Like a massive supercomputer, it must run at high efficiency to prevent overload. It does this by developing shortcuts, or educated guesses, based on what it already knows.

Shortcuts in the brain are created to help us understand information quickly. Since it is rarely possible to completely isolate one sense at a time, input from all the senses—vision, hearing, touch, taste, and smell—adds new information to the brain at the same time. That's a lot!

In this case, to help streamline the information, your brain has grouped these pictures together and compared them against images it already knows. For example, your brain knows that a circle looks like this:

A triangle looks like this:

So when your brain groups the pictures together, it fills in the lines that are missing. This is the most logical picture to your brain. Only when you really focus on the picture and tell your brain the triangles aren't there can you see the image as it really is.

But where does the brain get its information? How do we know what a triangle or circle looks like? We receive input from many sources, from both inside and outside the brain. Sights, sounds, touch—they all tell us something about our environment and ourselves.

One of the most complex senses is vision. Scientists believe this is because sight has always been a way for us to keep ourselves safe, find food, and navigate more easily through life.

Almost one-third of your brain is used to understand vision. But are we even seeing what we think we are seeing? Let's find out.

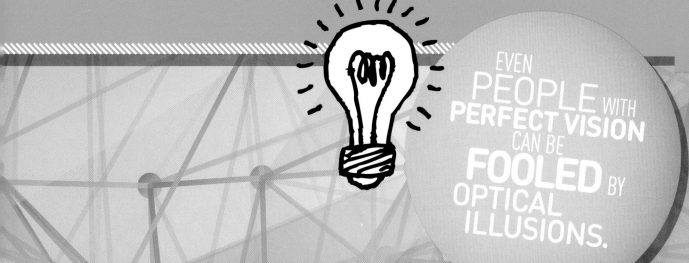

EVEN PEOPLE WITH PERFECT VISION CAN BE FOOLED BY OPTICAL ILLUSIONS.

RED LIGHT, GREEN LIGHT

Did you know that how your brain interprets color is as important as the image your eyes see?

CHALLENGE

What color is the apple? You probably said gray. But perhaps your brain thought green or red. That's because your brain isn't just seeing the color that's there. It's also interpreting it. Information stored in your visual cortex makes you imagine that the apple is red or green—even though it is actually gray.

Here's another one. What is this? Did you guess a stop sign? How did you know?

HOW YOU SEE COLOR

Light waves bounce off images and are sent to a layer of tissue that lines the back of your eye. It's called the retina. Within the retina are tiny cells, or photoreceptors, that are sensitive to light. These are known as rods and cones. Rods show us the world in black and white. They help us determine the shape of the object we see. Cones allow us to see color. The cones in your retina are sensitive to three main colors: red, green, and blue. The rods and cones send signals to your brain, which interprets the signals into colors and shapes.

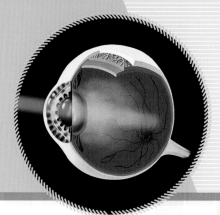

WHAT EXACTLY IS HAPPENING?

With both the apple and the stop sign, your brain saw the image and reviewed what it knows about it. That's why you thought the apple was red, even though it was gray. And how you knew the red octagonal sign meant "stop." This is another shortcut your brain takes. Your brain sees the color or shape, recognizes it instantly and tells you what the object is.

[MIND MATTERS]

HOW ANIMALS SEE COLOR

DOGS CAN ONLY SEE IN SHADES OF YELLOW TO BLUISH GRAY. Snakes see heat signatures of other animals. Pigeons see millions of different colors. The human brain can identify more than one million colors.

BLUE IS THE MOST COMMON FAVORITE COLOR. ONE STUDY FOUND **40%** OF ADULTS PICK BLUE AS THEIR MOST-LIKED COLOR.

OBJECTS MAY APPEAR CLOSER THAN THEY ARE

Vision:
Now in 3-D!

CHALLENGE

Stare at the flowers. Do any of them look like they are coming out of the picture at you?

WHAT EXACTLY IS HAPPENING?

You probably said the yellow ones. Actually, neither of the flower types in the picture is in 3-D. Your brain just thinks one is.

We are 3-D beings living in a 3-D world. But guess what? Our eyes can't see in 3-D. They only see in 2-D, or width and height. Your brain adds the depth. It uses highlights and shadows around an object to determine its depth. The yellow flowers look like they are in 3-D because they have extra lines around them that give them what looks like a shadow.

Humans rely on both eyes to see in 3-D. This is called binocular vision. Binocular vision is the blending of two different pictures—one from each eye—into one image.

THE EYES HAVE IT

Where the eyes are found on an animal determines the range of what they can see. Humans have two eyes positioned directly forward. This allows us to compare images seen in both eyes and enhance our 3-D vision. Animals with eyes on the sides of their head, like dogs, have a wider range of vision. But this makes their 3-D vision less reliable since both eyes are not seeing the same thing.

PEOPLE WITH STRABISMUS, COMMONLY KNOWN AS LAZY EYE, HAVE TROUBLE SEEING DEPTH.

CHALLENGE

**Hold a book at arm's length.
Close your left eye. Now close your right eye.**

WHAT EXACTLY
IS HAPPENING?

Your eyes see each image separately and send a signal to the visual cortex in the occipital lobe of the brain. The images are merged into one and you can see one book in its proper place in space. 3-D vision is important. Without it, we might be constantly bumping into things, not walking around them.

MIND MATTERS
DO THE PIGEON

DID YOU KNOW THAT PIGEONS BOB THEIR HEADS TO SEE BETTER? Pigeons also use an eye trick for 3-D vision. By bobbing its head, a pigeon's eyes take in multiple pictures of its surroundings. These images are processed by the pigeon's brain and create a 3-D image that the pigeon can understand.

CHALLENGE

Which brain seems to be raised above its background? The red or the blue?

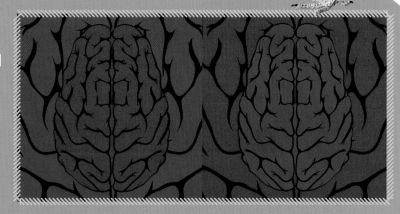

WHAT EXACTLY
IS HAPPENING?

You probably said the red one. That's because different colors focus at slightly different depths in the eye. Red has a longer wavelength than blue. Your eye has problems focusing on both wavelengths at the same time, so the blue becomes fuzzy. This makes your brain think the red is jumping out at it. This effect is called chromostereopsis (CHROME-oh-STAIR-ee-op-sis). And it is used to make a lot of 3-D movies.

WHEN YOU PUT ON A PAIR OF 3-D GLASSES, EACH EYE IS RECEIVING A DIFFERENT IMAGE. One image might be red and the other one green. Or sometimes one image is red and the other image is blue. The difference in the wavelengths makes your brain think it is seeing depth. The images are superimposed, or placed on top of each other in your brain, which is why when you take your glasses off, the picture appears blurry.

MIND MATTERS
GET OUT YOUR GLASSES

ALL ROADS LEAD TO THE FRONT

Sights, smells, sounds—all get passed through one hot spot.

Your brain takes in information from all of your senses and puts it to use. How? By creating neural pathways.

Signals from your senses come in from all over your body. Pictures from your eyes, sounds from your ears, and feeling anywhere you have skin. These signals all get sent to your brain's relay center, the thalamus. Then they get sent on to where they're processed.

Our sense of hearing, for example, allows us to get information from the world around us. But, like every other sense, the brain combines what it hears with what it may already know.

Your brain processes sounds in the auditory cortex, a part of the temporal lobe. When you hear music, nerves fire in your auditory cortex, just above your ear. Signals shoot along the neural highway to the frontal lobe.

Whether through sight, sound, touch, taste, or smell, new information constantly pours into your brain. Like a never ending cycle, this information creates new neural pathways every minute of every day.

Smells begin in the olfactory system, which includes your nose. Those signals are sent to the piriform cortex of the temporal lobe. Next they head to the thalamus and on to the frontal cortex, where you finally "smell" the smell. Other signals are sent even deeper to where memories live. That's why a smell can evoke such strong emotions.

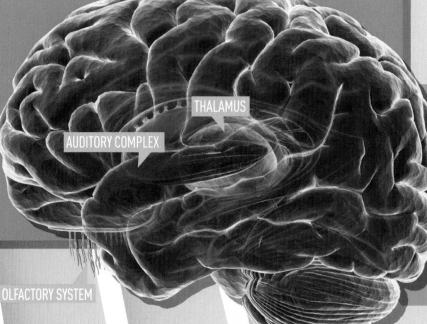

KING SNAKES CAN HEAR VERY QUIET SOUNDS BY FEELING VIBRATIONS IN THEIR JAWS.

THALAMUS

AUDITORY COMPLEX

OLFACTORY SYSTEM

[MIND MATTERS]
DOG-SNIFF-DOG WORLD

A DOG'S BRAIN IS LESS THAN ONE-TENTH THE SIZE OF A HUMAN'S, but the part that processes smells is almost 40 times bigger. That makes a dog's sense of smell 1,000 to 10 million times as sensitive as a human's. Dogs rely heavily on their sense of smell to understand their environment—and other dogs. When dogs sniff each other, it's their way of saying hello, kind of like how humans say "hi" or shake hands.

NEURO NOTES

Sniff! Smell that? Chances are, if you smell a smell, you know what it is. Sounds like a piece of cake, right? Here's how it works: Smells begin in the olfactory organ (the nose) and travel to the olfactory cortex in the temporal lobe. Taste travels via cranial nerves from the mouth to the thalamus and then on to the sensory cortex, known as the insula, where flavor is identified. The combination of taste and smell triggers an emotional response. Now, who wants cake?

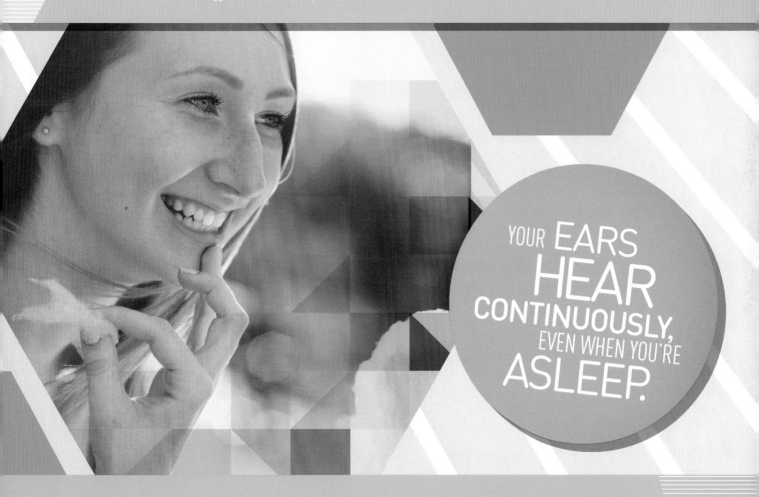

YOUR EARS HEAR CONTINUOUSLY, EVEN WHEN YOU'RE ASLEEP.

[MIND MATTERS]
EARWORMS

EVER HAVE A SONG STUCK IN YOUR HEAD? You might know the first line of the song, but the second one escapes you. No worry, says your brain. It simply replays the first line over and over. Scientists call this an earworm. Basically your brain is stuck in a loop. Your brain doesn't like to leave things unfinished, so it keeps going back over the first line in the hope that you will be able to finish the song. Unfortunately, that rarely happens. What can you do to end the loop? Read a book. Or solve a math problem. Using the analytical part of your brain is usually enough to kick you out of the loop.

THE CRANIUM EXPRESSWAY

Your brain houses an amazingly complex transportation system. Neural signals fly from one end to the other, navigating the cerebral superhighway at speeds not allowed on regular roads. If a signal encounters a gridlock, it shifts gears and heads another direction, or it goes off and makes its own road. New pathways are formed every time our brain learns something. But to maintain efficiency, your brain needs to store information it already knows somewhere. Think of it as a garage for your car. This information is called memories. So get ready, get set, we're about to take a jaunt down Memory Lane.

PAGE 14

A **THOUGHT** IS AN ELECTRICAL SIGNAL THAT TRAVELS ALONG **NEURAL CELLS.**

DID YOU CATCH THESE THOUGHTS?

PAGE 16
YOUR BRAIN TAKES **SHORTCUTS** WHEN IT **PROCESSES** THOUGHTS.

PAGE 22
THE **THALAMUS** IS THE BRAIN'S RELAY CENTER.

BRAIN BREAKS

1. WHAT DOES THIS PICTURE MEAN?

F R I E N D
D F
N R
E I
I E
R F D N

2. THE BOX PICTURED HERE HAS BEEN FOLDED TOGETHER FROM ONE OF THE FOUR CHOICES GIVEN. WHICH ONE?

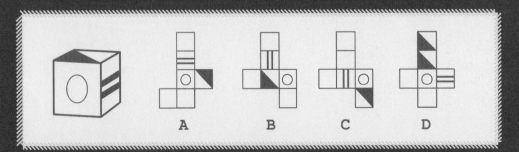

A   B   C   D

ANSWERS: 1. A CIRCLE OF FRIENDS; 2. D; 3. THE LETTER W; 4. 13 (DID YOU FORGET THE BIG TRIANGLE?) 5. 87, THE PICTURE IS UPSIDE DOWN.

Whew! That's a lot of information. Give your brain a break with these fun games.

3. WHAT IS AT THE END OF A RAINBOW?

5. WHAT IS THE NUMBER OF THE PARKING SPACE CONTAINING THE CAR?

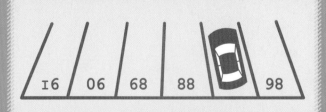

4. HOW MANY TRIANGLES ARE IN THIS PICTURE?

CHAPTER TWO

DOWN MEMORY LANE

Wish you had access to the largest storage system in the world? You do. Turn the page for an inside look at how the brain makes memories. →

FINDING THE ROUTE

You store mounds of memories in your brain. Find out how they stick around.

CHALLENGE

Start singing the ABC song. Did you get it right? Most people learn that song when they are very young. But you don't sing it every day, so why was your brain able to recall it?

WHAT EXACTLY IS HAPPENING?

Your brain stores memories. A memory is the snapshot of an event, feeling, or even a person that you have experienced before. The hippocampus is in charge of memory storage. But memories are actually stored all over your brain. Think of your brain as a huge city. The frontal, parietal, and occipital lobes are the surrounding towns, but all roads lead to the city center: the hippocampus.

Neurons are the communication network of the brain. Without them, you couldn't think, remember, or even walk. When neurons receive input from the senses, they "fire." It's like pushing a start button. An electrical signal is activated and sent zipping along the cerebral superhighway. It's looking for other neurons across the brain to connect with. No road to follow? No problem. Neurons just make new connections (or roads) as they go. That's called learning.

A memory is created when neurons fire in a specific pattern.

IT IS A 3-STEP PROCESS:
1) The first neuron receives the input.
2) The first neuron shoots the information to a second neuron, creating a new link.
3) Neurons shoot information to each other, creating a memory. Whether the memory sticks around depends on how often those neurons are fired again in that specific pattern.

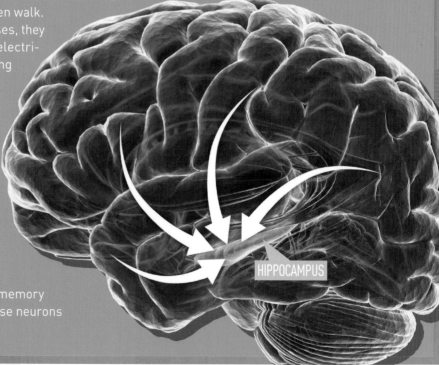

HIPPOCAMPUS

"PRACTICE MAKES PERFECT!" If you play an instrument or participate in a sport, you've probably heard that a million times. Practicing an action forces the neurons to shoot signals along the same "roads" over and over.

CHALLENGE

Sing the ABC song ... backward. Come on. You can do it. Z,Y,X ...
    How far did you get? Did you have to sing it forward in your head first to figure out the next letter? If you did, you are not alone.

WHAT EXACTLY IS HAPPENING?

Learning the ABC song made your neurons fire in a specific order. By trying to remember the song backward, you are forcing the neurons to create a new memory road. They don't like that. The memory pattern you have is to sing the song forward. The neurons don't know how to find the letters when you sing them backward. That is why you have a hard time singing the "ZYX" song.

LEARNING
ACTUALLY
CHANGES THE
PHYSICAL MAP
OF YOUR
BRAIN.

NEURO NOTES

Memories are stored as tiny bits of information all across your brain. For example, you may remember people by their hair or eye color, how they stand, or even how they smell. Each of these individual memories is stored by itself and in a different place. The color may be stored in your visual cortex and the smell in your olfactory cortex. As you remember, all of the separate memories come together to form one big picture of the person.

MEMORIES CAN TRIGGER OTHER MEMORIES. Remembering an old dog can make you think of his leash, how he smelled, how soft his fur was, even the park where you took him for walks. But it can also make you think of a dog bowl. And your neighbor's yard, where your dog dug a hole. And how your neighbor got angry at the hole. All these memories are linked together.

CHECK YOUR MEMORY

How much can your brain remember? Put it to the test.

CHALLENGE

Read this list three times. Then cover it.
Now get a pencil and a piece of paper. Write down the words you remember. How many did you get right? Five? Eight? Three?
If you are like most people, you may have gotten five to seven of the words. But how did your brain manage to remember any of these words at all?

CHAIR	RAINBOW	BUTTERFLY
CLOCK	COMPUTER	APPLE
HOUSE	SCISSORS	GLOBE
GUITAR	LIGHTBULB	HAMMER

WHAT EXACTLY IS HAPPENING?

Your brain has two types of memory: short-term and long-term. Short-term memory lasts anywhere from 15 to 30 seconds. Sometimes even up to a minute. That's about the time it takes for your computer to restart. Long-term memory is anything you can remember for longer than that.

When you read through the list, one loop of neurons went back and forth from the visual cortex to the frontal cortex. Another loop went from your auditory circuit to the frontal cortex. The hippocampus acts like the middleman. It shuttles information from your short-term memory to your long-term memory and back. In fewer than 15 seconds, a short-term memory was created.

HIPPOCAMPUS

MIND MATTERS
TYPES OF MEMORY

YOUR BRAIN SORTS MEMORIES INTO TYPES, INCLUDING:
EPISODIC memories are things that already happened, and include input from emotions and the senses.
SEMANTIC memories consist of facts, like your homework.
PROCEDURAL memories involve your actions, such as riding a bike.
WORKING memories include information that you need right away, like planning, organizing, and paying attention.

CHALLENGE

Take 30 seconds. Memorize as many of these pictures as you can. Cover the picture. Now get a pencil and a piece of paper. Write down the pictures you remember. How many did you get right? If you go back and look, you will see that these are pictures of the words in the last challenge. Did you get more of them right this time? Why?

WHAT EXACTLY IS HAPPENING?

Looking at pictures actually helps your brain to remember better. Short-term memory, also called working memory, relies heavily on the visual cortex. Words that are read are processed very quickly by our brains. They don't stick around for very long. But recording a picture in your brain takes longer. The more time spent looking at the picture, the better the memory. Saying a word out loud does the same thing. It takes longer to speak a word than it does to read it. That's why you remember it better when you say it aloud. The lesson? When you are doing last-minute cramming for a test, look at pictures and speak things out loud.
You memory—and your test score—will thank you.

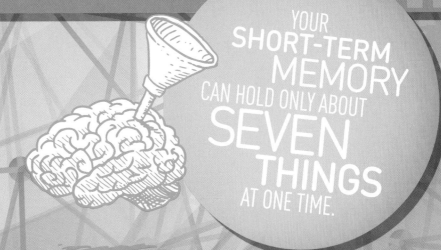

YOUR SHORT-TERM MEMORY CAN HOLD ONLY ABOUT SEVEN THINGS AT ONE TIME.

→IN REVERSE

Ah, memories. Trying to remember something? Let your senses be your guide.

CHALLENGE

Think back at least three years or more. Try to remember a time when you did something outside. Went to a park. Climbed a mountain. Maybe went bike riding.

See if you can answer these questions:

How warm or cold was it? What did it sound like? Who was with you? How did it smell?

You probably could answer them all, and maybe even remember more things. You may have even felt warm or cold like you did on that day. How can a memory that is three years old feel as if it's happening right now?

WHAT EXACTLY IS HAPPENING?

You are recalling a long-term memory. Long-term memories take a long time to form. They are also pretty complex. Unlike a short-term memory, emotions, sights, sounds, touch, taste, and smell all play a part in forming a long-term memory. Long-term memories are vivid. That's why you can remember the smells, the temperature, and probably whether you were happy or sad that day. Long-term memories can last for life.

THE SENSE OF **SMELL** CAUSES SOME OF THE **STRONGEST** MEMORY CONNECTIONS.

MIND MATTERS
FORGETTING HELPS TO REMEMBER

CAN FORGETTING ACTUALLY HELP YOU REMEMBER THINGS? Yes. Forgetting helps keep your mind uncluttered. Your memory is bombarded with details. If it tried to remember everything, it would overload. Instead, it simply forgets the small stuff and keeps the big things. It's a great system, actually. Be honest. Do you really need to remember what you had for lunch on January 15 two years ago?

NEURO NOTES

HOW A LONG-TERM MEMORY IS FORMED:

ATTENTION If something captures your attention, the thalamus knows about it. Neurons fire in the thalamus and zip along the superhighway to the frontal lobe, letting them know there is action that you need to watch.

EMOTION When you need an emotional reaction, the amygdala (a-MIG-da-la) sets up a memory pathway. Signals are blasted across the brain to areas that will keep the memory fresh.

SENSES Sight, sound, touch, taste, and smell will trigger a response in the brain. Neurons travel to the hippocampus and instruct it to form a memory from the sensory input.

STORAGE Like a computer, the hippocampus is a storage and retrieval center. It collects the data from all of the brain systems and processes the data into a long-term memory.

WHEN YOU SEE A PERSON, YOUR BRAIN GATHERS **ALL THE INFO** YOU KNOW ABOUT HIM OR HER.

MIND MATTERS
DID I DO THIS BEFORE?

YOU'RE HEADING TO A NEW PLACE FOR THE FIRST TIME. Suddenly, you have a strong feeling that you've been there before. But you **know** you haven't. Is your brain trying to trick you? No. You are experiencing déjà vu (DAY-ja VOO). Déjà vu happens when something in the new place or action triggers an old memory. The place or action feels familiar, even though you've never been there or done that before.

RECOGNITION RANGE

An image isn't always what it appears to be. Look close. Now, look closer.

CHALLENGE

What do you see here? A vase? Or two faces? Your brain can't decide, can it?

WHAT EXACTLY IS HAPPENING?

Your brain is hardwired to recognize faces. The urge is strong to see a face, but will it see one that isn't there? Give it another try.

CHALLENGE

What is this a picture of? Did you say a face? Actually, it's a picture of a faucet and two handles for hot and cold.

WHAT EXACTLY IS HAPPENING?

Your brain saw the image and recognized parts of a face. This is called the pareidolic (pair-eh-DOLL-ic) reaction. Faces are recognized in the fusiform gyrus, located just below your hippocampus. When the fusiform gyrus sees an image that looks like a face—eyes, nose, and a mouth—it reacts. Neurons fire and signals cruise to your frontal cortex. You see a face. Even if it isn't a real one.

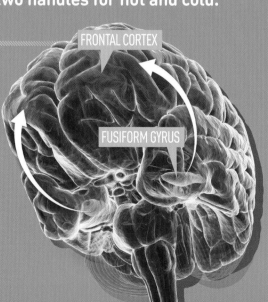

FRONTAL CORTEX

FUSIFORM GYRUS

MIND MATTERS

YOUR FACE IS YOUR PASSWORD

LIKE YOUR BRAIN, A COMPUTER CAN BE PROGRAMMED to pick out certain features to identify a person. Eye color, nose shape, size of mouth, color of hair, all are features the computer focuses on. Information is scanned and stored in memory. When the computer sees the person again, it compares the stored image against the live image. If they match, the person is identified. The funny thing is, most people can do this from birth, but it took engineers over 60 years to teach a computer to do it!

NEURO NOTES

Prosopagnosia (prahs-oh-pag-NO-shah), or face blindness, is a condition in which people cannot recognize faces. People with prosopagnosia may be unable to recognize new people, people they know, or even themselves in a mirror. Scientists believe that people who experience injury to the fusiform gyrus, the part of the brain that "sees" a face, may experience face blindness. It can happen because of a stroke, an injury to the head, or a disease such as Alzheimer's or dementia.

YOUR BRAIN STORES UP TO 2.5 PETABYTES OF KNOWLEDGE— THAT'S ENOUGH TO STORE 300 YEARS OF TV SHOWS.

PATTERN PARKWAY

Recognizing patterns is your brain's way of navigating through life.

CHALLENGE

Look at the pattern. What shape comes next?

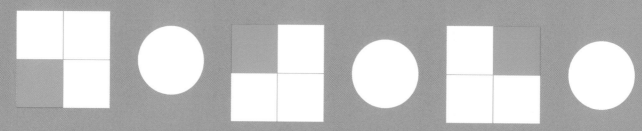

Did you say this one?

Then you are correct! But how did you know?

WHAT EXACTLY IS HAPPENING?

The same pareidolic reaction that causes you to see faces also helps you to see patterns. It works for shapes, colors, and even math problems. Patterns help the brain make sense of all of the information it receives. Much of the information input your brain receives is in bits and pieces, like the snapshot of a camera. By creating a pattern, the brain recognizes where the information "fits," almost like a piece into a big puzzle. The faster the brain sees the pattern, the faster it can understand the input and respond to it. Seeing patterns is a good thing. It helps us become aware of our surroundings and navigate through life.

MIND MATTERS

CAN YOU HEAR ME?

EVERYONE HAS AN INTERNAL NAVIGATION SYSTEM. It's your brain's way of moving about the world by recognizing patterns. But your internal navigation system does not just rely on sight. Other senses help. In fact, people who are without sight are able to rely primarily upon hearing to walk around. Memories help orient you to your surroundings, particularly if you've been somewhere before. Your brain will remember the "map" it created in your head the last time you visited and refer to that.

NOTE

WE ARE MORE LIKELY TO **REMEMBER INFORMATION** IF IT IS PROVIDED IN A **WEiRd** OR **UNUSUAL** FORMAT.

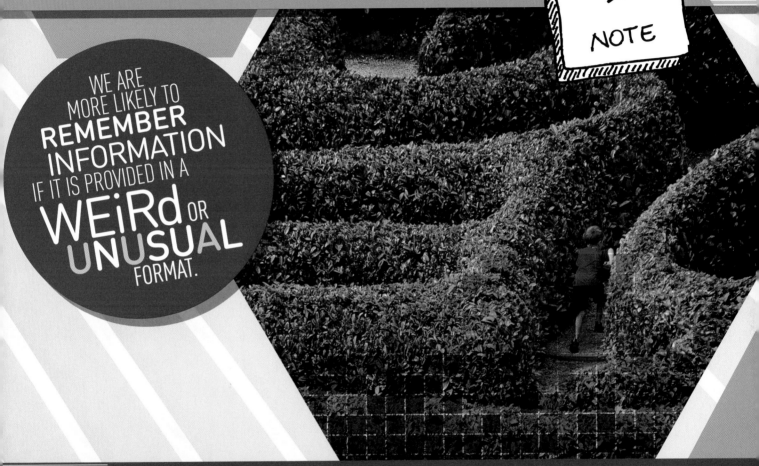

MIND MATTERS

LONG-LOST PETS

PETS HAVE A WAY OF RECOGNIZING PATTERNS, TOO. Ever heard those stories of lost pets that travel across the country to find their owners? Scientists believe that some types of animals have a "mental map" stored in their memory. They access the map and combine it with their keen sense of smell. It helps them track back to their neighborhood.

ROCKY TRAILS AHEAD

Memories are the road maps revealed by the brain. They help us know the places we've been, the things we've done and seen, and the people we've met along the way. Like all maps, however, memories can be faulty and need to be updated. That's why your hippocampus works in overdrive, constantly keeping your memory map fresh and new. But to move through life, you must go forward. It's time to take what we know and use it to branch out into new directions.

Fasten your seatbelt, we are about to hit the Emotion Expressway!

PAGE 30

THE **HIPPOCAMPUS** IS YOUR **MEMORY** BOSS.

DID YOU CATCH THESE THOUGHTS?

PAGE 31
LEARNING ACTUALLY **CHANGES** THE PHYSICAL MAP OF YOUR BRAIN.

PAGE 33
LOOKING AT **PICTURES** IMPROVES YOUR **MEMORY**.

NOTE

BRAIN BREAKS

1. WHICH PIECE FITS INTO THE PUZZLE?

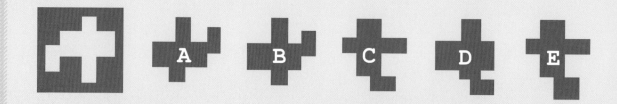

A   B   C   D   E

2. WHICH WAY IS THE BUS GOING?

ANSWERS: 1. C; 2. LEFT, THE DOOR IS ON THE OTHER SIDE; 3. BUMBLE BEE, PAPER CLIP, 4. EITHER, DEPENDING ON HOW YOU LOOK AT IT; 5. THEY'RE ALL THE SAME LENGTH.

Can you remember all that? Give your brain a break with these fun games.

3. WHAT DO THESE WORDS SAY?

elmbub ebe

repap plic

4. IS THE LADY IN THIS ART OLD OR YOUNG?

5. WHICH LINE IS LONGEST?

CHAPTER THREE

EMOTION EXPRESSWAY

Feeling happy? Feeling sad? Get in the mood to learn about how your brain deals with emotion. →

TWO-WAY TRAFFIC

There's more than just one part of your brain at work when you feel an emotion.

CHALLENGE

Look at this picture. How does it make you feel?

How does this picture make you feel?

Did looking at these pictures make you feel the urge to pick up the puppy or the baby and give it a hug? Why? What you are experiencing is called an emotion. Emotions are the way your brain expresses itself. Like the horn on a car, they are a way to communicate with others. Emotions are a response to a stimulus, something we experience in the world around us. They play a huge part in how we interact with others and ourselves. But how can simply looking at a picture make us feel an emotion?

NEURO NOTES

The amygdala and the hippocampus have a special nerve fiber connection that ties them together. It is a neural network that allows them to directly exchange information. Afferent (aff-er-rent), or input, fibers carry information from the hippocampus to the amygdala. Efferent (eff-er-rent), or output, fibers carry information from the amygdala back to the hippocampus. As signals fly back and forth, the brain is able to understand and interpret emotion quickly.

WHAT EXACTLY IS HAPPENING?

Emotions are formed in the limbic system, the middle part of the brain. The limbic system is known as the "feeling and reacting brain." It is responsible for the emotional response to things we see, feel, taste, hear, or smell. The main processor of the limbic system is the amygdala. Think of it as a big traffic director. The amygdala receives information via the neural superhighway and then tells the body how to react. The amygdala tells your brain when to feel scared or happy. It tells you when to feel stress or anger, and pretty much any other kind of emotion possible.

But the amygdala doesn't act on its own. It sends out signals via its own neural network to other parts of the brain, including the hippocampus. Each memory in the hippocampus has an emotion attached to it. The amygdala takes the emotional signal from the hippocampus, identifies it, and decides on a response. The response then cruises via a two-way traffic highway to the frontal cortex, or the thinking brain. For example, you see a puppy. Your brain's response is to make you feel happy and want to pick it up.

But your brain doesn't just send a single response. Signals fly back and forth continuously between the amygdala and the frontal cortex. This allows your brain to constantly review how it is reacting emotionally to the world around you.

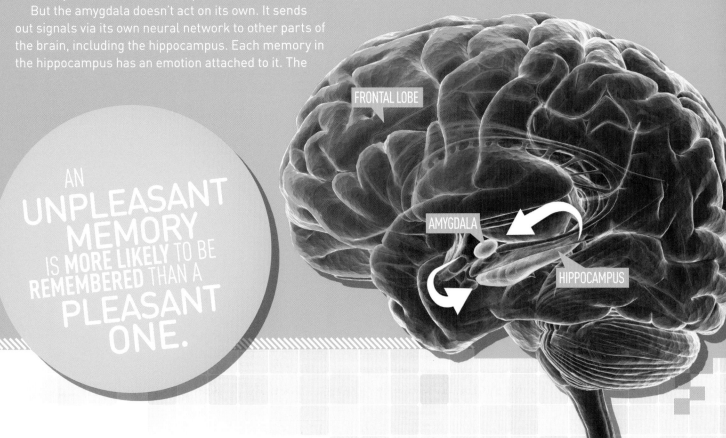

AN **UNPLEASANT MEMORY** IS **MORE LIKELY** TO BE **REMEMBERED** THAN A **PLEASANT ONE.**

FRONTAL LOBE

AMYGDALA

HIPPOCAMPUS

TURN SIGNALS

A change in facial expression can signal a change in emotion.

CHALLENGE

Look at these pictures. How do they make you feel? Happy? Sad? Grossed out?

WHAT EXACTLY IS HAPPENING?

The picture of the boy with the pie in his face may make you laugh out loud. Or maybe it makes you sad because you wanted to eat the pie. The picture of the girl watching the bug on her fork may gross you out. Totally! While happiness, sadness, and even a total gross-out feel very different, your brain represents them in a similar way. Your prefrontal cortex designs a neural code that represents each emotion. Neurons are designated as either positive or negative. A pattern is created for each emotional reaction. If the pattern has more positive neurons, then you feel happy. If the pattern created has more negative neurons, you feel sad, or another negative feeling like grossed out. *Blech.*

The interesting thing is that everyone has very similar neural codes. So if you look at the picture on the left and smile and so does your friend, chances are that you have created the same neural code in your brain. Cool, huh?

CHOCOLATE CONTAINS COMPOUNDS THAT RELEASE **ENDORPHINS,** OR HAPPY-MAKING CHEMICALS, IN OUR BRAINS.

PEOPLE FEEL SIX MAIN EMOTIONS: happiness, disgust, fear, surprise, anger, and sadness. You can feel just one emotion or many of them at one time. Emotions are complex. For instance, happiness can make you feel love, joy, or hope. And surprise can make you happy ... or fearful. But fear and surprise can lead to anger—or even happiness. It all depends if the surprise is a good one or not.

SOME ANCIENT PEOPLE BELIEVED **HAPPINESS** CAME FROM THE **HEART,** **ANGER** FROM THE **LIVER,** AND **FEAR** FROM THE **KIDNEYS.**

[MIND MATTERS]

ANIMAL EMOTIONS

ANIMALS HAVE EMOTIONS, TOO. Dogs smile and look happy when they are having fun. Sometimes they laugh. Scientists have recorded dog laughter and played it back for other dogs. It helped calm them. Young chimpanzees and orangutans laugh, too, when they are tickled under their armpits. Even rats have been known to laugh when they are tickled.

HA HA HA

READY FOR ACTION

Certain situations can really rev your engines, or cause a surge of emotion.

CHALLENGE

Imagine this crawling up your arm.

How did you react to that image?
Maybe it made you want to do this.

If seeing that giant spider made you feel like screaming, running, or waving your arm up and down, you are not alone. Many people respond to spiders that way. Your brain saw that spider and reacted—quickly and strongly. But why?

WHAT EXACTLY IS HAPPENING?

Scientists believe that emotions are designed to push us away from danger or toward a reward. In imagining the spider climbing up your arm, your brain perceived a direct threat. The amygdala is specially designed to deal with threats. One of the strongest emotions we feel is fear. When the amygdala senses fear, it shifts into high gear and turns on the body's panic system.

The amygdala shoots a lightning-fast signal to the hypothalamus, the organ that controls the internal workings of your body. When the neural signal hits your hypothalamus, instantly your heart beats faster, your eyes open wide, your stomach clenches, and your breathing speeds up. You are scared!

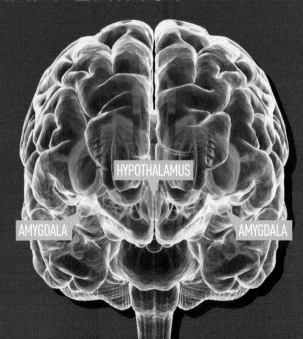

HYPOTHALAMUS

AMYGDALA   AMYGDALA

[MIND MATTERS]

PUT ON THE BRAKES!

PEOPLE JUMP AT YOU YELLING "SURPRISE!" All of a sudden, your heart is pounding, your chest is heaving, and your body is trembling. All they wanted to do was wish you a happy birthday. Who pushed your body's panic button? Your amygdala. It's not able to distinguish between a real threat and a perceived one. It felt you were in danger, so it set your body up to react. Once your brain realizes what is going on, it puts the brakes on the panic response.

NEURO NOTES

When stress is too much to handle, your body shifts into panic mode. You may feel as if you are trapped with no way out, and that can lead to a full-on panic attack. During a panic attack, your mouth becomes dry, your heart beats wildly, you may sweat, feel faint or dizzy, and even feel nauseous. Removing yourself from the problem that has upset you, taking deep breaths, and concentrating on calming down can help. And always be sure to let a parent, adult, or medical professional know.

[MIND MATTERS]

LOOK OUT BEHIND YOU!

THE FIGHT OR FLIGHT RESPONSE IS AN AUTOMATIC REACTION. When the amygdala shifts into panic mode, the thinking brain is bypassed. That means that your frontal cortex may not even realize what is happening until it senses your heart race and your stomach clench. Keep that in mind the next time you feel startled by a loud noise behind you. Blame it on your amygdala.

A CRYING BABY ACTIVATES OUR FIGHT OR FLIGHT RESPONSE.

Your fears may lead you to run and hide, but that's not all they do.

CHALLENGE

Memorize as many of these images as you can in ten seconds. How many did you get?

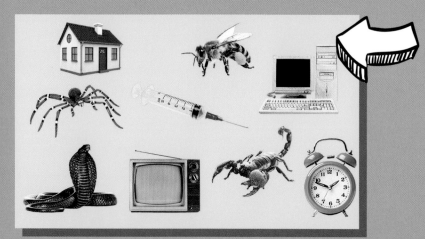

Now try the same thing with these images. Did you remember more from this set of images? Why?

WHAT EXACTLY IS HAPPENING?

Fear actually improves your memory. Scary items like the cobra, scorpion, spider, bumblebee, and syringe could have triggered your fight or flight reaction. When you experience fear, your senses become hyper-aware. You are on the alert. You are very aware of everything around you and ready to move at a moment's notice. Even just looking at a picture of something scary can trigger this reaction.

[MIND MATTERS]

PASS IT ON

RESEARCH SHOWS THAT IF YOU MAKE YOURSELF SMILE, in a few seconds you will start to feel happy. Don't believe it? Give it a try. Smile. Count to 10. Do you feel happy? You should. Or at least maybe you feel a little better. Try it for a longer time and see what happens. This also works if you want make someone else smile. Just go around with a big smile on your face and see how many people smile back at you. You will probably be surprised at the number.

THE STRONGER THE **EMOTION FELT** AT THE TIME OF **AN EVENT,** THE MORE LIKELY A PERSON IS TO **REMEMBER IT.**

[MIND MATTERS]

FREEZE!

EVER HEARD THE SAYING, "FROZEN WITH FEAR"? It can happen. Sometimes an intense scare makes you freeze. You can't move ... at all. Scientists believe this response is left over from our ancient ancestors. It was their way of staying safe by keeping still so that a predator would not see them. Since predators respond to movement, staying frozen is a great way to avoid being eaten.

COMPETITION CITY

Would you rather win or lose?
The answer is pretty simple.

CHALLENGE

Imagine you are in this race. Where do you want to see yourself?

Are you in the front of the pack or in the back? You probably said the front.

Here's another one. Which ribbon would you rather have?

You probably said first place, didn't you? Come on. Be honest. Most of us would want to win first place. Why? The brain wants to win! For most of us, competition is something our brain cells crave.

FIRST PLACE

SECOND PLACE

THIRD PLACE

KIDS AS YOUNG AS **4 YEARS** OF AGE UNDERSTAND **COMPETITIONS** AND WANT TO **WIN** AT THEM.

NEURO NOTES

Feeling good? That's probably because dopamine was released by the hypothalamus in response to a stimulus. That stimulus can be something good that happens, like a reward or a motivation, or it can be when you want to move around. When released, it gives your brain instructions. It can make you feel happy, impulsive, cautious, and even helps to control your movements. Higher levels of dopamine can reduce memory, attention, and problem solving in parts of the brain.

WHAT EXACTLY IS HAPPENING?

The brain loves rewards. It likes to feel it has accomplished something. The bigger the reward, the more your brain likes it. Which is why when you get a ribbon you feel good.

The hypothalamus, which regulates the function of your internal organs, really likes competition. When you compete, it releases a substance called dopamine (DOPE-a-meen). Dopamine is a neurotransmitter. That means it's a special chemical messenger that zips along from one neuron to another. Once released, the dopamine gives a sort of jolt to the neurons in the frontal cortex. The jolt is one your frontal cortex really likes. In fact, it likes it so much, that it wants more. That is why we keep competing. It makes us happy.

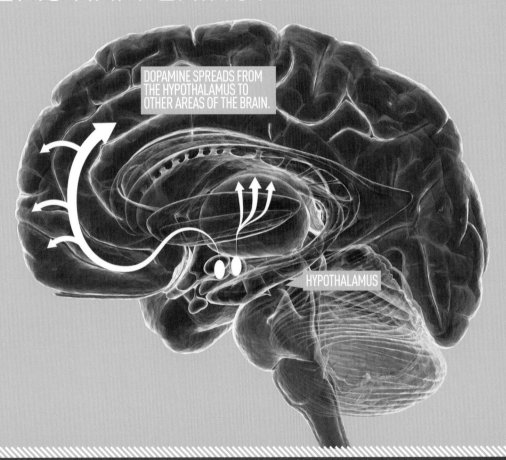

DOPAMINE SPREADS FROM THE HYPOTHALAMUS TO OTHER AREAS OF THE BRAIN.

HYPOTHALAMUS

GET YOUR BRAIN IN SHAPE!

GIVE YOUR BRAIN A WORKOUT—OF THE MENTAL KIND. The U.S. Olympic Committee's team of mental health professionals recommends the following brain boosters to keep your cranium in tip-top shape.
1. LEARN TO RELAX: Take a deep breath and feel the calm spread through your brain and body.
2. VISUALIZE: Close your eyes and see yourself performing the activity you plan to do. Go through every part of it and, most important, see yourself succeeding.
3. FOCUS: Block out all distractions and concentrate on the task ahead.
4. TRUST IN YOURSELF: You've done this before, you can do it again. OR if this is your first time performing, then trust that you've prepared well for your event.

ENTERING THE
STRESS ZONE

Feeling clammy, nervous, and anxious? That's stress.

CHALLENGE

What would make you more stressed?

Having to do a timed test, or ...

performing in front of an audience?

Believe it or not, both are forms of competition. One is competition with yourself and your classmates for a good grade. The other is a competition for your best performance. So, which would you choose? It's up to you. Some people think taking a test is horrible. Others are not bothered by it. But those same people who shrug at a test may feel their knees knocking and their hands shaking at the thought of performing in front of an audience. Participating in a sports event or a music competition creates stress. Why does stress bother us so much?

[MIND MATTERS]
PEAK PERFORMANCE

ATHLETES WHO COMPETE ARE USED TO BEING IN A CHALLENGE STATE. Some even welcome it. The sheer excitement of a challenge gets people motivated to compete. The athlete feels excited. His heart beats faster; his blood pumps rapidly through his veins. He is ready for competition. It makes him feel alive and ready to perform to his best ability. Let's go!

LAUGH OUT LOUD

Want a surefire way to relieve stress? Laugh out loud. It's no joke. Laughing is one of the best stress relievers around. When you laugh, your lungs fill with air, your heart speeds up a little, and your brain releases chemicals called endorphins that make you feel happy. These actions cause your muscles to relax, and you feel less stressed.

WHAT EXACTLY IS HAPPENING?

When you are under stress, your brain gets excited and you become anxious. But not all stress is bad. This isn't the hair-raising race to get out of there, fight or flight response. Instead, your body is in a challenge state. In a challenge state, your body is on alert status. It's primed and ready for action. Focused and prepared to meet any trial it encounters.

Just like in the fight or flight response, the hypothalamus handles the challenge state type of stress, too. The hypothalamus is your stress regulator. Think of it as a joystick on a remote control car. When you push down really hard, the car speeds up. When the hypothalamus is in a threat state, it goes to maximum and creates a fight or flight response. But when you just tap on the gas pedal, you get more of a moderated response. That is how the hypothalamus views a challenge state. It still sends messages to your lungs, heart, and muscles, but they are less frantic. It's kind of a heads-up, there's something that requires a lot of attention here.

In a challenge state your brain becomes more aware of its surroundings, your heart may pump a little faster, and your hands may even sweat, but you are nowhere near panic mode. You are focused. Your anxiety level may be up, but it's not so high that you feel the need to run screaming from the room.

WHEN YOUR BRAIN IS STRESSED YOU CAN EASILY FORGET THINGS, LIKE WHAT YOU WERE SUPPOSED TO DO FOR HOMEWORK.

EMOTIONS ON THE MOVE

Emotions can make you feel like you are all over the map. One minute you are heading down Happiness Lane and the next second you've swerved onto Anger Avenue. The amygdala traffic cop works overtime trying to keep your emotions running smoothly and efficiently. But like all systems, it can't work alone. Other parts of your brain must step up and help. Hold on to your thinking caps, we are about to take a trip down Decision Drive!

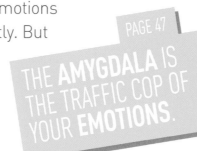

PAGE 47

THE **AMYGDALA** IS THE TRAFFIC COP OF YOUR **EMOTIONS**.

DID YOU CATCH THESE THOUGHTS?

PAGE 54
YOUR BRAIN LIKES **COMPETITION** AND LOVES TO WIN.

PAGE 51
YOUR BRAIN HAS A BUILT-IN PROTECTION UNIT—IT'S CALLED **FIGHT OR FLIGHT.**

FIRST PLACE

PANIC

BRAIN BREAKS

1. WHICH WEIGHS MORE, A POUND OF FEATHERS OR A POUND OF BRICKS?

2. IS THE CIRCLE INSIDE THE LARGER CIRCLE PERFECTLY ROUND OR IS IT MISSHAPEN?

ANSWERS: 1. NEITHER, THEY BOTH WEIGH ONE POUND. 2. IT'S PERFECTLY ROUND, TRACE IT WITH YOUR FINGER TO SEE; EVEN THOUGH YOUR BRAIN MAY THINK THEY ARE CURVED, THEY ARE STRAIGHT. 4. RIGHT BETWEEN THE I'S (EYES); 5. IT'S IMPOSSIBLE TO TELL, THIS IS AN OPTICAL ILLUSION.

Have some fun! Give your brain a break with these fun games.

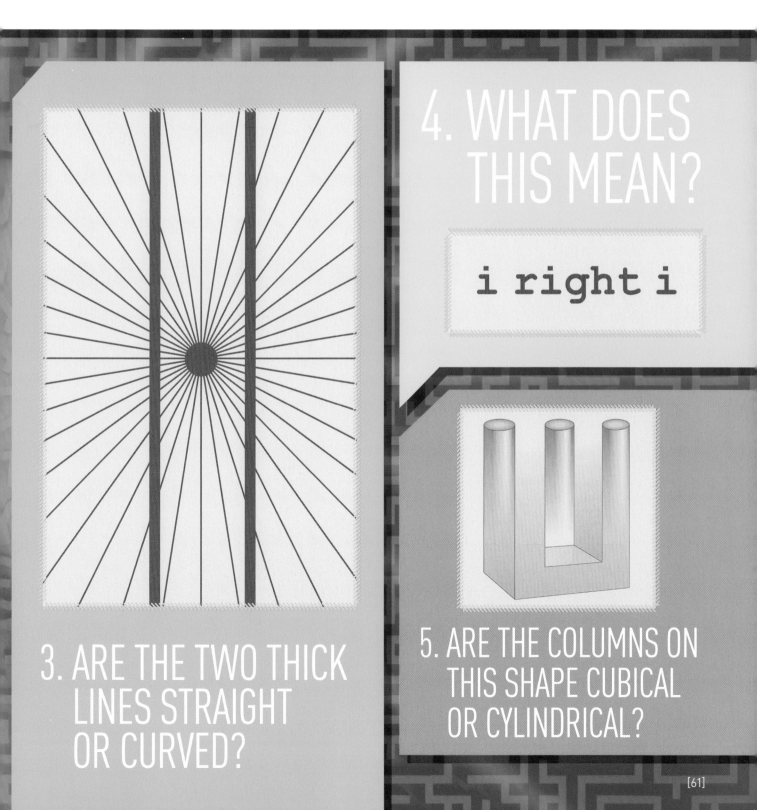

4. WHAT DOES THIS MEAN?

i right i

3. ARE THE TWO THICK LINES STRAIGHT OR CURVED?

5. ARE THE COLUMNS ON THIS SHAPE CUBICAL OR CYLINDRICAL?

[62]

CHAPTER FOUR
DECISION DRIVE

Decisions, decisions ... You make a million of them a day. Get set to see how the brain really makes choices. $\longrightarrow$

→LOGIC COURT

When faced with a decision, your brain gets to work.

CHALLENGE

What would you do if someone handed you this—and then told you that you have to pick one of these options:

OPTION 1: flip a coin to get either $100 more **OR** lose everything.

OPTION 2: get an extra $50 by doing nothing at all.

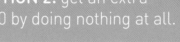

Which one do you pick?
New research suggests that if you are like most people, you will probably pick option 2. Sure, it's less money than option 1, but there's also less risk. Your brain doesn't like risk. It goes for the sure thing.

WHAT EXACTLY IS HAPPENING?

Your brain has two different decision-making processes: cognitive (COG-nih-tiv) control and value-based control. The cognitive thought group is like the family car. It's a slow and careful decision-making process, plodding along through life. It doesn't take risks, but instead carefully weighs every decision before making it. You are consciously aware of cognitive thought, which means you know the decision that you are making.

Value-based decisions, however, are more like a shiny race car. Your brain zooms through the decision-making process. It doesn't take the time to weigh the pros and cons of the decision. It makes decisions on the spot. As quick as snapping your fingers—bang—you've decided. Value-based decisions are unconscious, meaning you may not even be aware of them—until after you've already made them. While this type of decision may sound

like a bad thing, it's not. Sometimes you just need to decide. Fast.

Both types of decision-making take place primarily in the prefrontal cortex, the very front of your brain. Different areas within the prefrontal cortex evaluate, or review, the information and your prior experiences. Finally, your brain reaches a decision.

When you are presented with the two choices above, which do you choose? It depends. Which decision-making process is doing the deciding? If your cognitive thought process decides, you pick option 2. Definitely. Why? It's the less risky option. Money is money, after all, even if it is a smaller amount, and your brain probably remembered a time it lost a coin toss. But if your value-based thought process is turned on, you may feel the urge to just choose option 1. Why not? You could have $200!

[MIND MATTERS]
HOLD IT!

WHEN YOU HAVE TO GO, YOU HAVE TO GO. RIGHT? What if not going to the bathroom helped you make a big decision more easily? Think it's crazy? Well, it's true. Dutch scientist Mirjam Tuk proved just that. People who felt the urge were more patient and chose to wait for a bigger reward, even though it took longer. Then, they probably excused themselves rather quickly.

NEURO NOTES

All decisions—whether value-based or cognitive control—are made in the frontal lobe of the brain. But did you know that each type of decision-making happens in a different part of the lobe? Scientists have done studies of people's brains by hooking them up to scanners. When a person is faced with a value-based decision, the part of the frontal cortex that controls value-based thinking "lights up." The corresponding thing happens with cognitive control.

NEW EVIDENCE SUGGESTS THAT OUR **FRONTAL LOBES** CONTINUE TO DEVELOP INTO OUR **20s.**

[MIND MATTERS]
HOW WE DECIDE

YOUR BRAIN RECEIVES INPUT FROM YOUR SIGHT via the occipital lobe and converts it into an electrical signal, or neural impulse. The neural impulse cruises along the cerebral superhighway to the parietal lobe. The parietal lobe adds in its own information and shoots the impulse on to the prefrontal cortex, or very front part of your brain.

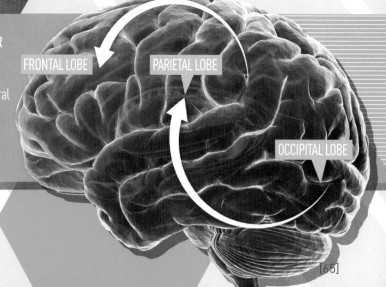

FRONTAL LOBE

PARIETAL LOBE

OCCIPITAL LOBE

[65]

→ DECISIONS, DECISIONS

Some are easy, and some are hard. Enter your brain's decision-making processes.

CHALLENGE

Which type of decision-making—cognitive or value-based—is this shopper using?

Both. (It was kind of a trick question.)

MONKEY SEE, MONKEY CHOOSE?

SCIENTISTS HAD TWO ADULT RHESUS MONKEYS WATCH A SET OF DOTS ON A SCREEN. Each monkey had to guess which way the dots would move. When a monkey guessed correctly, it got a reward. But, if it was wrong, it got nothing. There was another choice. The monkeys could choose the dots at the bottom of the screen and get an immediate, but smaller, reward. So what happened? If the monkeys felt good about their choice, they would go for the big score. But if they didn't, they went for the guaranteed treat. See, your brain isn't the only one that doesn't want to lose.

WHAT EXACTLY IS HAPPENING?

Every time your brain gears up to make a decision, both processes kick in. Your brain operates best when both the cognitive and value-based processes work together. Take grocery shopping. The cognitive process keeps you on track. It makes sure that the cereal you pick is good for you, that it's one you like, and one you want to eat.

The value-based process is more impatient. It may tell your brain, "Come on, just pick a cereal, already, because—ooo—look! those chocolate chip cookies over there are on sale! Cookies are much tastier than cereal!" You need both types of decision-making to get through the store.

[MIND MATTERS]
DECIDING TO STAY THIRSTY

VALUE-BASED THINKING COMES DOWN TO INSTINCTS. It's how we behave naturally. For example, giraffes need water to survive. But they won't drink at a pond or lake if they feel threatened. Why not? They have to bend down so far to drink that they are easy targets for any nearby predator. If they sense a predator in the area, they will decide to skip the drink and keep walking.

MOOD MANOR

Think logic rules your choices? Think again. Memories also have a say.

CHALLENGE

You take a seat between these two people. Which one would you decide to talk to?

Probably the boy on the right. Why? Your brain has decided he would be more open to speaking with you.

WHAT EXACTLY IS HAPPENING?

Your prefrontal cortex is the chief decision-maker. But like all good leaders, it wants everyone's input before it decides. That's why the input is run past the amygdala and the hippocampus. The amygdala checks the information for an emotional link, while the hippocampus filters it through your memory storage. Bam! If they get a hit, the neuron signals shoot through the superhighway to the frontal cortex. Then the frontal cortex adjusts its decision based on their feedback.

The reason why you picked the smiling boy to talk to is because your amygdala told you that smiling people are happy people. So chances are, he'd like to talk to you, too. Your frontal cortex told your brain that talking with this boy would be a good experience. So you turn to him and say "hi."

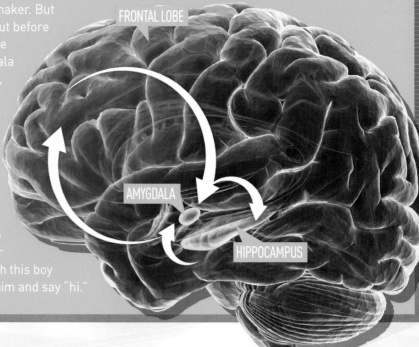

FRONTAL LOBE

AMYGDALA

HIPPOCAMPUS

CHALLENGE

Does this look like a fun place to go on vacation?

What if looking at that picture reminded you of the time you got this?

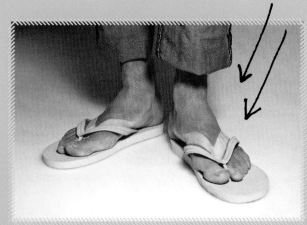

Seeing the picture of the sunburn may have changed your mind. Why?

WHAT EXACTLY IS HAPPENING?

Your brain related the beach with the memory of the sunburn. Ouch! You may have even cringed as the memory was replayed in your brain. Chances are, you won't decide to go back to the beach. At least not without lots of sunblock!

Emotions and memories play a huge part in our decisions. Happier memories make us want to do things. But painful or sad memories make us decide to avoid things. It all depends on how your frontal cortex interprets the information it receives from the amygdala and the hippocampus.

[**MIND MATTERS**]

GOTCHA!

YUM! DON'T THESE BANANAS LOOK GOOD? Why? The front bananas stand out compared with the overripe one, making them more appealing. That's known as the decoy affect. Advertisers use this technique to play on your emotions. If one choice seems better, then you are more likely to decide to buy it.

ANGER CAN CAUSE YOU TO MAKE DECISIONS QUICKLY— AND NOT ALWAYS CORRECTLY.

HEAVY TRAFFIC

When there are just too many options to consider, it's decision overload!

CHALLENGE

Which would you pick for breakfast? Come on. Choose. Your brain is weighing the pros and cons of each. The donut is delicious, but the oatmeal is better for you. Find yourself torn between the two? You are not alone. Most people not only can't decide, but also feel anxious and worried about their choice.

WHAT EXACTLY IS HAPPENING?

Your brain is constantly bombarded with decisions. Do you have an orange or a banana for a snack? How about ice cream? But what flavor? Should I take swimming lessons or learn piano? This type of information overload, or multitasking, can actually produce the opposite effect. When faced with the constant demand for decisions, you can start to feel, well ... indecisive. That means you can't make a decision at all. And that's not good.

When that happens, your brain starts creating shortcuts. It makes decisions on autopilot. It even makes things up. You think you want to learn to swim. Sure. Your brain agrees. Your brain likes to take the time to figure things out. But when push comes to shove, it will make a decision. Although, it's not always the best one or the one you really wanted.

MIND MATTERS

CRANK THOSE TUNES!

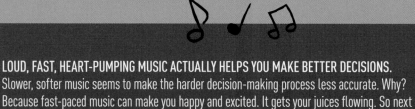

LOUD, FAST, HEART-PUMPING MUSIC ACTUALLY HELPS YOU MAKE BETTER DECISIONS. Slower, softer music seems to make the harder decision-making process less accurate. Why? Because fast-paced music can make you happy and excited. It gets your juices flowing. So next time you are faced with a tough decision, crank up the tunes and put on some music to move to. It will make your mind shake, rattle, and roll to the right decision.

GO WITH WHAT YOU KNOW

Which of these would make a great spokesperson for a book on history? You probably said George Washington. When given an option between choosing someone you know and someone you don't, your brain will almost always pick the familiar object. Why? It's comfortable. You know this person—or know of him. He's famous. For some reason, that makes it easier for you to choose. So, when in doubt, your brain goes with what you know.

PEER PRESSURE CAN AFFECT PEOPLE OF ANY AGE.

CHALLENGE

Pick an ice cream flavor. Did you pick your favorite? Now consider this, ten of your friends chose the same flavor, BUT it was different from your choice. Do you feel the urge to change your pick?
Many people would.

WHAT EXACTLY IS HAPPENING?

You are experiencing peer pressure. Peer pressure is when a group of people, similar in age, background, and interests, try to influence a person's decisions. It can be obvious. For example, a person tells you to pick the strawberry flavor, because the cool kids eat only strawberry. Or it can be subtle. Everyone else picks the strawberry flavor and you pick it, too, just because they did.

Why did you pick the same flavor as everyone else? You wanted to fit in. People who go along with the crowd are perceived to be better liked than those who stand out and make their own decisions. That isn't true. Making your own decisions doesn't mean you don't want to be liked, just that you want to be an individual. Don't get caught up just following the pack because it's easy. Stand out and let your decisions be heard.

→ SHIFTING GEARS

So much to do, so little time. Enter multitasking.

CHALLENGE

Say the colors of these words out loud.

BLUE	RED	ORANGE	BROWN
PINK	GREEN	YELLOW	TAN
GRAY	WHITE	PURPLE	BLACK

Did you get them right? Or did you start reading the word instead of saying the color?

WHAT EXACTLY IS HAPPENING?

Your brain got mixed up while trying to complete this task. You were asking it to do too many things at once. It has to do with speed and attention. When you read, Wernicke's area, the part of the brain that handles speech, processes the word quickly. But the color of the word is processed more slowly, in the occipital lobe. The race is on! Which bit of information will reach your frontal cortex first? Whichever one does will be what your brain decides to do first: read or say the color. Since your brain reads faster than it can identify color, and since your brain has learned that, usually, what the word says is more important than how it looks, reading wins. That's why you end up reading the word instead of saying the color. This is called the Stroop Effect.

Try it again. Really concentrate this time:

BLUE	RED	ORANGE	BROWN
PINK	GREEN	YELLOW	TAN
GRAY	WHITE	PURPLE	BLACK

Did you do any better? If so, you probably had to slow down. Saying the colors required more time and attention. But it may still have been hard. You may have even had to work hard to override what your brain told you first.

TOO MANY THINGS TO DO? Remember the rule of 20. Your brain works more efficiently if you concentrate on each task for no more than 20 minutes. Give it a try. Take a deep breath. Set the timer. Go! Twenty minutes of work. Now stop. Take another deep breath. On to the next task. You will find that you accomplish more this way. Your brain cells will thank you.

NEURO NOTES

Scientists use the Stroop Effect to understand how well your brain evaluates information. By taking the Stroop test, scientists can determine if your brain processes colors or words faster. This knowledge could help you when studying for an exam. If the Stroop test shows you are a visual person, then paying attention to visual cues will help you remember information best. But if you are a words person, you will do better with writing.

THE **BRAIN** CAN HANDLE **2** **COMPLEX TASKS** **AT ONCE,** BUT JUGGLING **3 OR MORE TASKS** IS DIFFICULT.

FRONTAL LOBE

WERNICKE'S AREA

OCCIPITAL LOBE

→SPLITSVILLE

When you're doing two things at once, your brain goes into overdrive.

CHALLENGE

Draw a circle with your left hand and AT THE SAME TIME draw a straight line with your right hand.

Could you do it? Probably not.

WHAT EXACTLY IS HAPPENING?

Multitasking splits the brain. Instead of allowing your brain to focus on one task at a time, you are forcing it to do two things at once. The prefrontal cortex must switch back and forth from one task to another. It speeds neuron signals first to the circle, then to the line, spending no more than a few seconds on each. That's why just as you felt you were making progress on the circle your brain stopped, switched gears, and concentrated on drawing the line. Talk about going in circles!

Try it again. Only this time, draw the circle first THEN draw the straight line.

Were you able to do it? Sure. You gave your frontal cortex time to focus on each task individually. What you may not realize is that you are multitasking in both challenges. They are just different forms of multitasking. The first is one in which you try to do tasks simultaneously. In the second challenge, you did two tasks but in succession, or one after the other. It's clear to see that the second challenge was easier. Maybe that's why we shouldn't do two things at once, like text and drive.

Multitasking can get a lot easier when one of the tasks is something you've done a million times. Tasks that you do all the time are recognized by your brain and are seen as learned tasks. Every time your brain needs to complete a learned task, it remembers what needs to be done and does it unconsciously. For example, think about walking up a flight of stairs at home or school. You don't need to think about taking each step, lifting your feet to the right height—your brain knows how high each step is from past experience. So, you can do other things while you walk—talk to a friend, read a book, watch a TV show. But if the height of the step is changed even a little bit, say because your parents installed a new carpet, you will probably trip if you are not paying attention. Time to retrain your brain!

REWARDS ARE A GREAT WAY TO **MOTIVATE** A TIRED BRAIN INTO **MAKING A DECISION.**

[**MIND MATTERS**]

VIDEO GAMES = BETTER BRAIN?

HOW MANY TIMES HAVE YOU HEARD THAT PLAYING VIDEO GAMES IS BAD FOR YOU? Turns out, that may not be the case. Playing action-based video games actually improves your decision-making process. Video gamers are more aware of their surroundings, better at multitasking, and even have faster response times. So charge up that controller and start pounding those keys. Who says gaming isn't an active sport? You are giving your brain a workout!

LEFT OR RIGHT?

Decisions. We can't get through life without them. The prefrontal cortex sits in the driver's seat and steers you through life. Whether planning, executing, or completing a task, nothing gets done until the prefrontal cortex decides it does. It single-handedly merges thought, emotion, and memories into a combined pit crew that preps and readies you for the decision-making process. With a countdown it sends you off to action! 3-2-1 get ready for take off to Action Avenue!

PAGE 64

YOUR BRAIN HAS TWO DIFFERENT **DECISION-MAKING** PROCESSES.

DID YOU CATCH THESE THOUGHTS?

PAGE 70
YOUR BRAIN TAKES **SHORTCUTS** WHEN IT BECOMES OVERLOADED WITH DECISIONS.

PAGE 68
EMOTIONS PLAY A BIG PART IN **DECISION-MAKING.**

BRAIN BREAKS

1. WHAT DO YOU SEE?

2. ARE THE HORIZONTAL LINES PARALLEL, OR DO THEY SLOPE?